Table Of Contents

Title: Mental Health Matters: Nurturing Emotional Well-being for All

In this subchapter, we will explore the importance of mental health and provide valuable insights on nurturing emotional well-being for everyone. Whether you are seeking to improve your overall health and wellness, enhance mindfulness and meditation practices, incorporate fitness and exercise into your routine, adopt healthier eating habits, manage stress effectively, prioritize mental health, or improve sleep and relaxation, this chapter is tailored to address all these niches.

Our emotional well-being plays a vital role in our overall health and happiness. Mental health encompasses our emotional, psychological, and social well-being, affecting how we think, feel, and act. By nurturing our mental health, we can better cope with the challenges life throws at us and enjoy a more fulfilling and balanced life.

Within these pages, you will find strategies and techniques to enhance your mental well-being. We will discuss the importance of incorporating mindfulness and meditation practices into your daily routine, providing you with tools to calm your mind, reduce stress, and improve focus and clarity.

Furthermore, we will explore the connection between physical health and mental well-being. Engaging in regular exercise not only improves physical fitness but also releases endorphins, the brain's natural feel-good chemicals. We will provide tailored exercise routines and tips to help you incorporate fitness into your lifestyle.

Nutrition and healthy eating habits are crucial for maintaining a healthy mind. We will guide you through the process of making nutritious choices that support your mental health and well-being. Additionally, we will delve into stress management and relaxation techniques, equipping you with practical methods to reduce anxiety, manage stress, and promote relaxation in your daily life.

Mental health deserves our attention and care. We will discuss various mental health issues, their impact on our lives, and ways to seek help or support when needed. We will emphasize the importance of self-care, self-compassion, and fostering healthy relationships to nurture emotional well-being.

Lastly, we will address the significance of sleep and relaxation in maintaining a healthy mind. Quality sleep is vital for mental and physical rejuvenation. We will explore techniques for improving sleep patterns and creating a restful environment.

This subchapter aims to empower you with knowledge and practical tools to nurture your mental health and emotional well-being. Regardless of your background or interests, the insights provided here are applicable to everyone. Remember, mental health matters, and by prioritizing it, you can lead a more vibrant and fulfilling life.

Chapter 1: Understanding Mental Health and Emotional Well-being

The Importance of Mental Health

In today's fast-paced and demanding world, it is crucial to recognize the significance of mental health. Mental Health Matters: Nurturing Emotional Well-being for All sheds light on the importance of prioritizing our mental well-being and offers practical strategies for achieving a balanced and healthy mind.

For individuals seeking overall well-being, mental health is a key component. It affects every aspect of our lives, from our relationships to our physical health. When our minds are healthy, we are better equipped to handle stress, make sound decisions, and maintain positive relationships. Mental health is not just the absence of mental illness; it is a state of well-being that allows us to thrive and reach our full potential.

In this subchapter, we delve into the various niches that are interconnected with mental health. Firstly, health and wellness. When we focus on mental health, we are more likely to adopt positive lifestyle habits that support our overall well-being. This includes engaging in regular physical exercise, eating a balanced diet, and practicing mindfulness and meditation techniques.

Mindfulness and meditation, one of the fastest-growing trends in the wellness industry, are invaluable tools for improving mental health. These practices promote self-awareness, reduce stress, and enhance emotional resilience. Incorporating mindfulness and meditation into our daily routines can have a profound impact on our mental well-being.

Fitness and exercise play a significant role in maintaining good mental health. Physical activity releases endorphins, which are known as "feel-good" hormones. Regular exercise not only improves our physical fitness but also boosts our mood, reduces anxiety, and helps us manage stress effectively.

Nutrition and healthy eating also contribute to mental well-being. Research suggests that certain nutrients, such as omega-3 fatty acids, B vitamins, and antioxidants, play a crucial role in maintaining optimal brain function. By adopting a balanced and nutritious diet, we can support our mental health and promote emotional well-being.

Stress management and relaxation techniques are essential for maintaining mental health in our fast-paced lives. In this subchapter, we explore various strategies to manage stress, including deep breathing exercises, engaging in hobbies, and setting healthy boundaries. These techniques help us recharge, reduce burnout, and maintain mental equilibrium.

Sleep and relaxation are fundamental to mental health. Quality sleep is essential for cognitive function, emotional well-being, and overall health. We delve into the importance of establishing healthy sleep habits, such as maintaining a consistent sleep schedule and creating a relaxing bedtime routine.

In conclusion, Mental Health Matters: Nurturing Emotional Well-being for All emphasizes the importance of mental health for everyone. By prioritizing mental well-being, engaging in mindfulness and meditation, adopting healthy lifestyle habits, managing stress effectively, and getting adequate sleep, we can cultivate a healthy mind and lead fulfilling lives. Remember, mental health matters, and investing in it is an investment in ourselves.

Defining Emotional Well-being

Emotional well-being is a fundamental aspect of overall health and happiness. It is a state of balance and resilience, where individuals are able to effectively cope with the daily challenges and stressors of life. This subchapter aims to provide a comprehensive understanding of emotional well-being, its importance, and how it can be nurtured for everyone.

Emotional well-being encompasses the ability to recognize and understand one's own emotions, as well as the emotions of others. It involves effectively managing these emotions and using them as a guide for decision-making and interpersonal relationships. Emotional well-being is not about being happy all the time, but rather about having the tools and resources to navigate the ups and downs of life with grace and resilience.

In today's fast-paced and often stressful world, it is crucial to prioritize emotional well-being. It impacts every aspect of our lives, from our relationships and work performance to our physical health and overall quality of life. By nurturing our emotional well-being, we can enhance our ability to cope with stress, build healthy relationships, and maintain a positive outlook even during challenging times.

To nurture emotional well-being, it is essential to adopt a holistic approach that integrates various aspects of health and wellness. This includes practices such as mindfulness and meditation, fitness and exercise, nutrition and healthy eating, stress management and relaxation techniques, mental health and emotional well-being, as well as sleep and relaxation.

Mindfulness and meditation can help individuals develop self-awareness and cultivate a sense of calm and presence. Fitness and exercise not only benefit physical health but also release endorphins that boost mood and reduce stress. Nutrition and healthy eating provide the necessary nutrients to support brain health and stabilize emotions. Stress management and relaxation techniques, such as deep breathing and progressive muscle relaxation, help individuals unwind and reduce anxiety. Mental health and emotional well-being awareness are vital in seeking help and support when needed. Lastly, prioritizing sleep and relaxation ensures that our bodies and minds have the time to rejuvenate and recover.

By actively engaging in these practices, individuals can enhance their emotional well-being and lead more fulfilling lives. This subchapter will explore each of these aspects in detail, providing practical tips and strategies for incorporating them into daily routines. It is a valuable resource for anyone seeking to prioritize their emotional well-being and create a life of balance, resilience, and happiness.

Common Misconceptions about Mental Health

In today's fast-paced world, it is essential to prioritize mental health alongside physical well-being. However, there are still many misconceptions surrounding mental health that often prevent individuals from seeking the help they need or fully understanding its importance. In this subchapter, we aim to debunk these misconceptions and provide valuable insights into mental health for everyone.

One common misconception is that mental health issues only affect a specific group of people. The truth is that mental health knows no boundaries and can impact anyone, regardless of age, gender, or background. It is crucial to recognize that mental health is a universal concern and that we all have a role in nurturing emotional well-being.

Another misconception is that mental health problems are a sign of weakness or personal failure. This harmful belief perpetuates stigma and prevents individuals from seeking help. Mental health issues are not a reflection of one's character or strength; they are medical conditions that require professional support and treatment. Understanding this can help create a more compassionate and supportive environment for those struggling with mental health challenges.

Additionally, there is a misconception that mental health is solely about mental illness. Mental health encompasses a broad spectrum, including emotional well-being, resilience, and overall psychological wellness. It is not solely focused on diagnosable conditions but also on promoting positive mental states and building psychological resilience to cope with life's challenges.

Another myth is that mental health problems cannot be prevented or managed effectively. On the contrary, there are numerous strategies and techniques available to improve mental health and prevent the onset of mental health issues. Engaging in regular exercise, maintaining a balanced diet, practicing mindfulness and meditation, managing stress, and prioritizing sleep are all effective ways to nurture emotional well-being.

Lastly, there is a misconception that mental health issues are temporary and will resolve on their own. Mental health should be treated with the same seriousness as physical health. Seeking professional help and support is crucial to recover and manage mental health conditions effectively.

By debunking these common misconceptions, we hope to create a better understanding of mental health for everyone. Mental health matters, and by nurturing our emotional well-being, we can lead healthier, happier lives. It is essential to prioritize mental health alongside physical well-being and to create a supportive environment that encourages open conversations about mental health for all.

Chapter 2: The Mind-Body Connection

Exploring the Mind-Body Connection

In this subchapter, we delve into the fascinating topic of the mind-body connection and its profound impact on our overall well-being. Understanding this connection is essential for everyone, as it can greatly enhance our mental health and emotional well-being.

The mind-body connection refers to the intricate link between our thoughts, emotions, and physical health. It highlights the fact that our mental and emotional states can directly influence our physical well-being and vice versa. When we nurture this connection and strive for balance, we can experience improved health, vitality, and happiness.

One powerful way to nurture the mind-body connection is through mindfulness and meditation practices. By cultivating present-moment awareness, we can become more attuned to our thoughts, emotions, and physical sensations. Through regular practice, we learn to observe without judgment and develop a deeper understanding of ourselves. This heightened self-awareness not only promotes mental clarity and emotional resilience but also positively impacts our physical health.

Fitness and exercise play a crucial role in the mind-body connection as well. Engaging in regular physical activity not only boosts our mood and reduces stress but also enhances our cognitive function. Exercise releases endorphins, the feel-good hormones that uplift our spirits and combat anxiety and depression. Additionally, being physically active improves cardiovascular health, strengthens muscles, and boosts our immune system.

Nutrition and healthy eating are integral to the mind-body connection. The food we consume directly affects our brain chemistry, mood, and energy levels. A balanced diet rich in whole foods, fruits, vegetables, and lean proteins provides the essential nutrients our bodies and minds need to function optimally. By fueling ourselves with nutritious foods, we can enhance our mental clarity, promote emotional stability, and maintain overall well-being.

Stress management and relaxation techniques are vital components of the mind-body connection. Chronic stress is detrimental to both our mental and physical health. By adopting stress management techniques such as deep breathing exercises, yoga, or taking regular breaks for relaxation, we can reduce stress levels and cultivate a sense of calm and balance.

Quality sleep is another critical aspect of the mind-body connection. When we sleep, our bodies repair, recharge, and consolidate memories. Adequate sleep is crucial for optimal cognitive function, emotional stability, and overall well-being. By prioritizing sleep hygiene and adopting relaxation techniques before bed, we can improve the quality of our sleep, enhance our mood, and increase our resilience to stress.

In conclusion, exploring the mind-body connection is essential for everyone seeking to nurture their emotional well-being. By incorporating mindfulness, fitness, nutrition, stress management, and quality sleep into our daily lives, we can embark on a transformative journey towards improved mental health and overall vitality.

How Mental Health Affects Physical Health

In today's fast-paced society, mental health is often overlooked or brushed aside, but it is crucial to understand that our emotional well-being has a direct impact on our physical health. This subchapter delves into the intricate relationship between mental and physical health and emphasizes the significance of nurturing emotional well-being.

The mind and body are inherently interconnected, and any imbalance in one can manifest in the other. Research has proven that individuals with poor mental health are more susceptible to physical ailments. Conditions such as chronic stress, anxiety, and depression can weaken the immune system, making us prone to infections and diseases. Moreover, mental health issues often lead to unhealthy coping mechanisms such as substance abuse, poor diet choices, and lack of exercise, further compromising physical well-being.

Stress, a prevalent issue in our society, plays a pivotal role in this mind-body connection. Chronic stress releases stress hormones like cortisol, which, when constantly elevated, can lead to numerous health problems, including heart disease, obesity, and diabetes. Therefore, it is crucial to manage stress effectively through various relaxation techniques and mindfulness practices.

Exercise and physical activity have been proven to be an excellent way to improve mental health. Engaging in regular fitness routines releases endorphins, the feel-good hormones, which help combat anxiety, depression, and stress. Additionally, exercise promotes better sleep and boosts self-esteem, leading to an overall improvement in emotional well-being.

Nutrition and healthy eating play an equally significant role in maintaining good mental health. Consuming a balanced diet rich in essential nutrients not only nourishes the body but also supports brain health. Certain foods like omega-3 fatty acids, found in fish and nuts, have been linked to improved mental well-being. Conversely, a diet high in processed foods, sugar, and caffeine can exacerbate mental health issues.

Sleep is another crucial aspect that should not be overlooked. Lack of sleep has a profound impact on mental health, increasing the risk of developing mood disorders and cognitive impairments. Prioritizing quality sleep and implementing relaxation techniques before bedtime can significantly improve mental and physical health.

By understanding the intricate relationship between mental and physical health, we can prioritize emotional well-being alongside physical fitness. Integrating mindfulness and meditation practices, exercise, healthy eating, stress management techniques, and quality sleep into our daily routines can contribute to a healthier and more balanced life. Remember, mental health matters, and nurturing it is essential for overall well-being.

Incorporating Exercise for Improved Mental Well-being

Exercise is not just beneficial for physical health; it also plays a significant role in improving mental well-being. In this chapter, we will explore the powerful connection between exercise and emotional well-being, and how incorporating physical activity into your daily routine can positively impact your mental health.

Regular exercise has been shown to release endorphins, which are known as "feel-good" hormones. These endorphins act as natural mood boosters and can help alleviate symptoms of depression, anxiety, and stress. Engaging in physical activity also increases the production of serotonin and dopamine, neurotransmitters that are responsible for regulating mood and promoting feelings of happiness and relaxation.

Apart from the chemical benefits, exercise can provide a much-needed break from our daily stressors. It offers an opportunity to redirect our focus and energy, allowing us to take a break from rumination and negative thought patterns. When we engage in physical activity, we become more present in the moment, providing a form of mindfulness that can greatly improve mental well-being.

Furthermore, exercise can help combat the effects of chronic stress. Stress has a detrimental impact on our mental health, leading to increased anxiety, irritability, and fatigue. Regular exercise acts as a buffer against stress, as it reduces the production of stress hormones such as cortisol and adrenaline. By incorporating exercise into our routine, we can effectively manage stress levels and improve our overall emotional well-being.

To reap the benefits of exercise for mental health, it is essential to find activities that you enjoy. Whether it's going for a brisk walk, practicing yoga, dancing, or playing a sport, finding something that brings you joy and gets you moving is key. Start small and gradually increase your activity level to avoid burnout or injury.

Incorporating exercise into your daily routine can be as simple as taking the stairs instead of the elevator, scheduling regular walks during your lunch break, or joining a fitness class with a friend. Remember that consistency is key, so aim for at least 150 minutes of moderate-intensity exercise per week.

In conclusion, exercise is a powerful tool for improving mental well-being. By incorporating physical activity into your daily routine, you can boost your mood, reduce stress, and enhance overall emotional well-being. So, put on your sneakers, get moving, and experience the transformative effects of exercise on your mental health.

Chapter 3: Mindfulness and Meditation

Introduction to Mindfulness

In today's fast-paced and demanding world, it is crucial to prioritize our mental well-being. Mental Health Matters: Nurturing Emotional Well-being for All aims to provide valuable insights and guidance for everyone interested in improving their emotional health. This subchapter, titled "Introduction to Mindfulness," introduces the concept of mindfulness and its profound impact on our overall well-being.

Mindfulness is the practice of being fully present in the moment, aware of our thoughts, emotions, and bodily sensations without judgment. It allows us to cultivate a sense of calm and clarity amidst the chaos of our daily lives. While mindfulness has roots in ancient Eastern traditions, it has gained significant popularity in recent years due to its scientifically proven benefits.

The health and wellness community has embraced mindfulness for its potential to reduce stress, increase self-awareness, and improve overall mental health. By integrating mindfulness into our daily routine, we can experience a greater sense of peace, contentment, and resilience.

Mindfulness and meditation go hand in hand, as meditation is a powerful tool for cultivating mindfulness. By dedicating a few minutes each day to meditation, we can train our minds to focus on the present moment, developing a heightened sense of awareness and concentration. Regular meditation practice has been shown to reduce anxiety and depression, enhance cognitive abilities, and promote emotional well-being.

Incorporating mindfulness into our fitness and exercise routines can also enhance our overall well-being. By bringing our awareness to our bodies' sensations during physical activity, we can deepen our connection to the present moment and foster a more profound mind-body connection. This can lead to increased enjoyment and improved performance in our workouts.

Additionally, mindfulness can positively impact our nutrition and eating habits. By practicing mindful eating, we can savor each bite, fully experiencing the flavors and textures of our food. This mindful approach to eating can promote healthier choices, prevent overeating, and improve our relationship with food.

Furthermore, mindfulness offers powerful techniques for stress management and relaxation. By developing a mindful mindset, we can navigate stressful situations with greater ease and respond to them in a more balanced way. Mindfulness-based stress reduction techniques, such as deep breathing exercises, body scans, and progressive muscle relaxation, can help us relax, reduce tension, and restore our mental equilibrium.

In conclusion, this subchapter on "Introduction to Mindfulness" serves as a gateway to understanding the transformative power of mindfulness in our lives. By embracing mindfulness, we can enhance our mental health and emotional well-being, improve our sleep and relaxation, manage stress effectively, and foster a greater sense of overall wellness. Stay tuned for practical tips and techniques to incorporate mindfulness into your daily routine in the upcoming chapters of Mental Health Matters: Nurturing Emotional Well-being for All.

Benefits of Practicing Mindfulness

In today's fast-paced and constantly evolving world, it is becoming increasingly important to prioritize our mental health and emotional well-being. One powerful tool that can help us achieve this is mindfulness. Mindfulness is the practice of intentionally paying attention to the present moment without judgment. It involves bringing our awareness to our thoughts, feelings, bodily sensations, and the environment around us. This subchapter explores the numerous benefits that practicing mindfulness can bring to our lives.

One of the most significant benefits of mindfulness is its positive impact on mental health and emotional well-being. Research has shown that regular mindfulness practice can reduce symptoms of anxiety and depression. By cultivating a non-judgmental attitude towards our thoughts and emotions, we can learn to observe them without getting caught up in negative spirals. This helps us develop resilience and better cope with stress and challenging situations.

Additionally, mindfulness can enhance our physical health. When we practice mindfulness, we become more attuned to our bodies' needs. This heightened awareness allows us to make healthier choices regarding nutrition and exercise. Mindfulness can also improve our sleep quality by reducing racing thoughts and promoting relaxation before bedtime.

Mindfulness is not limited to a specific time or place; it can be incorporated into our daily activities. By bringing mindfulness into our eating habits, we can savor each bite, eat more mindfully, and make better food choices. This practice can help us develop a healthier relationship with food and prevent overeating.

Regular mindfulness practice also improves our ability to manage stress. By becoming aware of our stress triggers and learning to respond instead of react, we can reduce the harmful effects of stress on our bodies and minds. Mindfulness techniques, such as deep breathing and body scans, can be utilized anytime, anywhere, to bring about a sense of calm and relaxation.

Moreover, mindfulness enhances our overall well-being by fostering a sense of gratitude and appreciation for the present moment. It allows us to disconnect from the constant stream of distractions and fully engage in our experiences. This heightened awareness brings more joy, contentment, and a greater sense of purpose to our lives.

In conclusion, mindfulness practice offers a multitude of benefits to individuals of all ages and backgrounds. Whether you are seeking to improve your mental health, enhance physical well-being, manage stress, or simply find more peace and happiness, incorporating mindfulness into your daily life can be transformative. By taking the time to cultivate mindfulness, we can nurture our emotional well-being and lead more fulfilling lives.

Different Meditation Techniques for Mental Health

In today's fast-paced and stress-filled world, taking care of our mental health has become more important than ever. One effective way to nurture emotional well-being is through meditation. Meditation is a practice that involves training the mind to focus and redirect thoughts, resulting in improved clarity, calmness, and overall mental well-being. In this subchapter, we will explore various meditation techniques that can benefit everyone, regardless of their age or background.

1. Mindfulness Meditation:
Mindfulness meditation involves paying attention to the present moment without judgment. It helps individuals become aware of their thoughts and emotions, allowing them to observe them without getting caught up in them. This technique is particularly helpful for reducing stress, anxiety, and depression, while promoting self-acceptance and compassion.

2. Loving-Kindness Meditation:
Loving-kindness meditation involves cultivating feelings of compassion, love, and kindness towards oneself and others. By focusing on positive intentions and well-wishes, this technique can enhance feelings of connection, empathy, and positivity. It is especially beneficial for building stronger relationships and reducing negative emotions.

3. Transcendental Meditation:
Transcendental meditation involves silently repeating a mantra, a specific word or phrase, to achieve a state of deep relaxation and inner peace. Regular

practice of this technique has been shown to reduce anxiety, improve focus and concentration, and enhance overall well-being.

4. Body Scan Meditation:
Body scan meditation involves systematically focusing attention on different parts of the body, noticing any sensations or tension present. This technique helps individuals develop body awareness, release physical tension, and improve their ability to relax deeply. It is particularly useful for promoting better sleep and reducing chronic pain.

5. Guided Visualization Meditation:
Guided visualization meditation involves creating vivid mental images that evoke a sense of relaxation, calm, and positivity. It helps individuals tap into their imagination and harness the power of positive thinking. This technique can enhance motivation, confidence, and overall mental clarity.

By incorporating these different meditation techniques into our daily lives, we can create a positive impact on our mental health and emotional well-being. Whether it's reducing stress, improving focus, or fostering self-compassion, meditation provides a powerful tool for achieving balance and peace of mind. So, take a few moments each day to explore these techniques and discover the transformative power of meditation.

Chapter 4: Nutrition and Healthy Eating

Understanding the Impact of Nutrition on Mental Health

Introduction:

In recent years, there has been growing recognition of the profound connection between nutrition and mental health. Our diet not only affects our physical well-being but also plays a crucial role in nurturing our emotional and mental well-being. This subchapter aims to shed light on the impact of nutrition on mental health, providing valuable insights for everyone seeking to enhance their emotional well-being.

The Mind-Body Connection:

The intricate link between our mind and body cannot be overstated. Nutritional deficiencies can lead to imbalances in brain chemistry, impacting our mood, cognition, and overall mental health. By understanding the role of nutrition in mental well-being, we can make informed choices to support our mental health.

The Power of a Balanced Diet:

A balanced diet rich in essential nutrients, including omega-3 fatty acids, B vitamins, and antioxidants, can positively influence mental health. These nutrients contribute to the production of neurotransmitters, such as serotonin and dopamine, which regulate mood and emotions. Including a variety of fruits, vegetables, whole grains, lean proteins, and healthy fats in our meals can provide the necessary nutrients for optimal mental health.

Gut Health and Mental Health:

Emerging research has unveiled the significant role of gut health in mental well-being. The gut-brain axis is a complex communication network between our gut and brain. A healthy gut microbiome, which is nourished by a diverse range of fibers and probiotics, can promote mental wellness and reduce the risk of conditions like anxiety and depression. Cultivating a gut-friendly diet can involve incorporating fermented foods, high-fiber foods, and reducing processed and sugary foods.

The Impact of Sugar and Processed Foods:
Consuming excessive amounts of sugar and processed foods can have detrimental effects on mental health. These foods can lead to inflammation, oxidative stress, and disrupt the balance of neurotransmitters, contributing to mood disorders and cognitive decline. It is crucial to be mindful of our sugar intake and opt for whole, unprocessed foods whenever possible.

Personalized Nutrition for Mental Health:
Every individual is unique, and so are their nutritional needs. Personalized nutrition, considering factors such as genetics, lifestyle, and specific mental health conditions, can optimize mental well-being. Collaborating with healthcare professionals, such as registered dieticians or nutritionists, can provide guidance on tailoring our diet to support our specific mental health goals.

Conclusion:
Understanding the impact of nutrition on mental health empowers us to take proactive steps in nurturing our emotional well-being. By adopting a balanced diet, prioritizing gut health, and being mindful of our food choices, we can support mental wellness and overall quality of life. Remember, the journey to emotional well-being starts with the plate in front of us.

Essential Nutrients for Emotional Well-being

In today's fast-paced world, where stress and anxiety seem to be ever-present, taking care of our emotional well-being has become crucial. While many factors contribute to our mental health, one area that often goes overlooked is the role of essential nutrients. In this subchapter, we will explore how certain vitamins and minerals can support our emotional well-being and provide practical tips on incorporating them into our daily lives.

1. Omega-3 Fatty Acids: These healthy fats are known to reduce inflammation and promote brain health. Research suggests that omega-3s, found in fatty fish like salmon and sardines, can help alleviate symptoms of depression and anxiety. If you are vegetarian or vegan, consider incorporating flaxseeds, chia seeds, or walnuts into your diet, which are rich in plant-based omega-3s.

2. B Vitamins: B vitamins play a crucial role in maintaining a healthy nervous system and brain function. Vitamin B12, in particular, is essential for mood regulation. Sources of B vitamins include whole grains, legumes, leafy greens, and lean meats. If you are unable to meet your daily requirements through diet alone, consider talking to your healthcare provider about supplementation.

3. Magnesium: This mineral is involved in over 300 biochemical reactions in the body, including those that regulate mood and reduce stress. Incorporate magnesium-rich foods like almonds, spinach, avocados, and dark chocolate into your diet. Alternatively, you can also try taking a magnesium supplement, especially if you experience symptoms of anxiety or insomnia.

4. Vitamin D: Known as the "sunshine vitamin," vitamin D plays a crucial role in our mental health. Low levels of vitamin D have been associated with depression and seasonal affective disorder. Spend time outdoors, especially during sunlight hours, to naturally boost your vitamin D levels. If you live in a region with limited sunlight, consider taking a vitamin D supplement or consuming fortified foods like milk and orange juice.

Remember, a well-rounded approach to emotional well-being includes not only proper nutrition but also exercise, stress management, mindfulness, and quality sleep. By incorporating essential nutrients into your diet, you are giving your mind and body the support they need to thrive. Consult with a healthcare professional or registered dietitian to create a personalized plan that suits your needs. Take charge of your emotional well-being today and embrace a healthier, happier you!

Developing a Balanced and Healthy Eating Plan

In today's fast-paced world, it's easy to neglect our diet and opt for quick, convenient meals that often lack the necessary nutrients our bodies need. However, maintaining a balanced and healthy eating plan is crucial for our overall well-being, both physically and mentally. By nourishing our bodies with the right foods, we can fuel our minds, boost our energy levels, and enhance our emotional well-being.

When it comes to developing a balanced and healthy eating plan, it's essential to focus on incorporating a variety of nutrient-dense foods into our daily meals. This means including a mix of fruits, vegetables, whole grains, lean proteins, and healthy fats. These foods are rich in vitamins, minerals, and antioxidants that can support our immune system, improve brain function, and reduce the risk of chronic diseases.

Mindfulness and meditation can play a significant role in developing a healthy eating plan. By practicing mindfulness, we can become more aware of our eating habits, such as recognizing when we're truly hungry versus eating out of boredom or emotions. Taking the time to savor our food, paying attention to its flavors and textures, can help us develop a healthier relationship with food. Additionally, incorporating meditation into our daily routine can reduce stress and emotional eating, allowing us to make more conscious food choices.

Physical fitness and exercise go hand in hand with a balanced eating plan. Regular physical activity not only helps maintain a healthy weight but also improves our mood and mental well-being. When we engage in exercise, our bodies release endorphins, which are natural mood boosters. Therefore, combining a balanced diet with regular exercise can have a positive impact on our mental health and emotional well-being.

Nutrition and healthy eating have a direct correlation to stress management and relaxation techniques. Certain foods, such as those rich in omega-3 fatty acids and magnesium, can help reduce stress and promote relaxation. Incorporating foods like fatty fish, nuts, seeds, and dark chocolate into our diet can provide these beneficial nutrients, helping us manage stress and promote a sense of calm.

Finally, a balanced and healthy eating plan can positively influence our sleep and relaxation patterns. Avoiding heavy meals close to bedtime and instead opting for lighter, easily digestible foods can improve sleep quality. Additionally, certain nutrients, such as tryptophan found in turkey, can promote a better night's rest. By prioritizing our diet, we can support a healthy sleep routine, which is essential for our overall mental health and emotional well-being.

In conclusion, developing a balanced and healthy eating plan is crucial for everyone. By incorporating a variety of nutrient-dense foods, practicing mindfulness and meditation, engaging in regular exercise, managing stress, and promoting better sleep, we can nurture our emotional well-being and achieve optimal mental health. Remember, small changes in our eating habits can lead to significant improvements in our overall quality of life.

Chapter 5: Fitness and Exercise for Mental Health

The Relationship between Fitness and Mental Health

In today's fast-paced world, it is becoming increasingly important to prioritize mental health alongside physical well-being. As we strive to live healthier and more fulfilling lives, it is essential to recognize the powerful connection between fitness and mental health. This subchapter aims to shed light on this relationship and provide valuable insights for everyone, regardless of their background or interests.

Physical fitness encompasses various aspects, including exercise, nutrition, sleep, and stress management. Each of these elements plays a crucial role in promoting mental well-being.

Exercise is not only beneficial for our physical health but also has a profound impact on our mental state. Engaging in regular physical activity releases endorphins, the brain's "feel-good" chemicals, which can reduce symptoms of anxiety and depression. Exercise also promotes better sleep, increases self-confidence, and provides a healthy outlet for stress and tension.

Nutrition and healthy eating are closely linked to mental health too. A well-balanced diet that includes essential nutrients, vitamins, and minerals helps support brain function and emotional well-being. By nourishing our bodies with wholesome foods, we provide the necessary fuel for optimal brain performance, enhancing our cognitive abilities and emotional resilience.

Another essential aspect of mental health is stress management and relaxation techniques. Chronic stress can negatively impact our mental well-being, leading to anxiety, depression, and other mental health disorders. Engaging in activities such as meditation, mindfulness, and deep breathing exercises can help alleviate stress, improve concentration, and promote a sense of calmness and peace.

Furthermore, proper sleep and relaxation contribute significantly to our mental health. Research has shown that a lack of sleep can impair cognitive function, increase irritability, and heighten the risk of mental health issues. Implementing healthy sleep habits and relaxation techniques, such as creating a soothing bedtime routine or practicing relaxation exercises before sleep, can enhance the quality of our sleep and boost our overall mental well-being.

Understanding the relationship between fitness and mental health is crucial for everyone. By incorporating regular exercise, healthy eating habits, stress management techniques, and quality sleep into our lives, we can nurture our emotional well-being, improve our mental resilience, and achieve a more balanced and fulfilling life.

In conclusion, this subchapter emphasizes the significance of the relationship between fitness and mental health. It encourages individuals from all walks of life to prioritize their mental well-being by incorporating fitness-related practices into their daily routines. By embracing a holistic approach to health and wellness, we can cultivate emotional well-being, reduce stress, and enhance our overall quality of life.

Choosing the Right Exercise Routine for You

In today's fast-paced world, finding the right exercise routine can be overwhelming. With countless options available, it's important to choose a workout plan that suits your needs, preferences, and goals. By selecting the right exercise routine, you can improve your overall well-being, physical health, and mental clarity. This subchapter aims to guide you in making an informed decision about the ideal exercise routine for your unique requirements.

When it comes to selecting an exercise routine, there are several factors to consider. First and foremost, you need to identify your fitness goals. Are you aiming to lose weight, increase strength, improve flexibility, or enhance your cardiovascular health? Understanding your objectives will help you choose the appropriate exercises that align with your goals, ensuring maximum effectiveness.

Additionally, it's important to consider your personal preferences. If you dread going to the gym, you may want to explore outdoor activities such as hiking, swimming, or cycling. On the other hand, if you prefer the structure and guidance of a fitness class, you could consider options like yoga, Pilates, or high-intensity interval training (HIIT). By choosing activities that you enjoy, you are more likely to stay committed and motivated in the long run.

Furthermore, it's crucial to consider your current fitness level and any physical limitations you may have. If you're a beginner or have certain health conditions, it's advisable to start with low-impact exercises, gradually increasing intensity and duration as you become more comfortable. Consult with a healthcare professional or a certified fitness trainer to ensure you choose exercises that are safe and suitable for your individual circumstances.

Remember that a well-rounded exercise routine should incorporate elements of cardiovascular exercise, strength training, and flexibility exercises. Aim for a balanced approach that includes activities like brisk walking, jogging, weightlifting, stretching, and yoga. By diversifying your workouts, you can target different muscle groups, prevent injuries, and maintain overall fitness.

Lastly, listen to your body and be flexible with your exercise routine. Your needs and preferences may change over time, and it's essential to adapt accordingly. Stay open to trying new activities, explore different classes or workout styles, and find what works best for you.

Choosing the right exercise routine for you is a personal journey. By considering your goals, preferences, fitness level, and overall well-being, you can create a workout plan that supports your mental, emotional, and physical health. Remember, the most important thing is to find joy and satisfaction in your exercise routine, as it will help you maintain long-term commitment further and holistic well-being.

Incorporating Exercise into Your Daily Routine

Physical activity plays a crucial role in maintaining and promoting overall well-being. Incorporating exercise into your daily routine can have numerous benefits for your mental health and emotional well-being, in addition to the obvious physical advantages. This subchapter aims to provide practical tips and guidance on how you can seamlessly integrate exercise into your busy schedule.

Exercise is not limited to intense workouts at the gym; it encompasses a wide range of activities suitable for people of all fitness levels and ages. Whether it's walking, jogging, swimming, dancing, or practicing yoga, finding an activity that you enjoy is key to making exercise a regular part of your life.

One effective way to incorporate exercise into your daily routine is by setting aside specific times for physical activity. This could be as simple as waking up half an hour earlier to go for a brisk walk, or dedicating your lunch break to a quick workout session. By treating exercise as a non-negotiable part of your daily agenda, you are more likely to stick to it and reap the benefits.

To make exercise even more enjoyable, consider involving friends or family members. Organize group walks, bike rides, or fitness classes together. Not only will this provide social interaction, but it will also create a sense of accountability and motivation among participants.

Additionally, integrating exercise into your daily routine doesn't have to be time-consuming. Small changes can make a big difference. For example, choose to take the stairs instead of the elevator, park your car a little further away from your destination, or perform stretching exercises during TV commercial breaks. These small actions add up over time and contribute to your overall fitness level.

Remember, exercise is not only about physical health; it also has a profound impact on mental well-being. Regular physical activity can reduce stress, anxiety, and depression, while improving mood, self-esteem, and cognitive function. By prioritizing exercise in your daily routine, you are investing in your mental health and emotional well-being.

In conclusion, incorporating exercise into your daily routine is essential for maintaining optimal health and well-being. By finding activities you enjoy, scheduling exercise time, involving others, and making small changes, you can seamlessly integrate physical activity into your life. The benefits extend beyond physical fitness, positively impacting your mental health, stress management, and emotional well-being. So, start today and make exercise a vital part of your daily routine for a healthier and happier life.

Chapter 6: Stress Management and Relaxation Techniques

Identifying and Managing Stress

Stress is an inevitable part of life that affects us all, regardless of age, gender, or background. It can manifest in various ways, such as feeling overwhelmed, anxious, or irritable. In order to nurture our emotional well-being, it is crucial to identify and effectively manage stress. This subchapter aims to provide practical strategies and techniques to help everyone lead a healthier and more balanced life.

Firstly, it is important to be aware of the signs and symptoms of stress. This can include changes in appetite, difficulty concentrating, trouble sleeping, or increased heart rate. By recognizing these indicators, we can intervene early and prevent stress from escalating. Additionally, being mindful of our emotional state allows us to better understand our stress triggers and take appropriate action.

Next, managing stress requires adopting positive coping mechanisms. One effective technique is practicing mindfulness and meditation, which involves focusing on the present moment and cultivating a non-judgmental awareness. Engaging in regular mindfulness exercises can help reduce stress, improve concentration, and promote emotional well-being. Similarly, incorporating exercise and physical activity into our daily routine can significantly reduce stress levels. Exercise releases endorphins, the body's natural mood boosters, and helps to alleviate tension and anxiety.

Nutrition also plays a vital role in managing stress. Consuming a balanced diet rich in fruits, vegetables, and whole grains provides essential nutrients and supports overall well-being. Avoiding excessive caffeine, sugar, and processed foods can help stabilize mood and energy levels. Additionally, incorporating stress-busting foods such as dark chocolate, green tea, and omega-3 fatty acids can be beneficial.

In order to effectively manage stress, it is crucial to engage in relaxation techniques. These can include deep breathing exercises, progressive muscle relaxation, or engaging in hobbies and activities that bring joy and relaxation. Taking breaks, setting boundaries, and practicing self-care are essential components of stress management as well. Lastly, ensuring adequate sleep and relaxation is crucial for emotional well-being. Establishing a regular sleep routine, creating a calming sleep environment, and practicing relaxation techniques before bed can greatly improve sleep quality and reduce stress levels.

By identifying and managing stress, we can cultivate emotional well-being and lead a balanced life. Incorporating mindfulness, exercise, nutrition, relaxation techniques, and quality sleep into our daily routine can significantly reduce stress levels and improve overall mental health. Remember, everyone faces stress, but with the right tools and strategies, we can successfully navigate through life's challenges and nurture our emotional well-being.

Effective Stress Management Techniques

In today's fast-paced and demanding world, stress has become an inevitable part of our lives. It can affect our mental health, emotional well-being, and even physical health if left unaddressed. However, by incorporating effective stress management techniques into our daily routine, we can significantly reduce the negative impact of stress and nurture our emotional well-being.

1. Mindfulness and Meditation: One of the most powerful ways to manage stress is through mindfulness and meditation practices. By focusing our attention on the present moment, we can cultivate a sense of calm and reduce stress levels. Regular meditation sessions, even as short as 10 minutes a day, can help us develop resilience and cope better with stressful situations.

2. Fitness and Exercise: Engaging in regular physical activity not only benefits our physical health but also plays a crucial role in managing stress. Exercise releases endorphins, the feel-good hormones, which can elevate our mood and reduce anxiety. Whether it's going for a brisk walk, practicing yoga, or hitting the gym, finding an exercise routine that suits our preferences is essential for stress management.

3. Nutrition and Healthy Eating: Our diet plays a significant role in managing stress levels. Consuming a well-balanced diet rich in fruits, vegetables, whole grains, and lean proteins provides our body with the necessary nutrients to combat stress. Avoiding excessive caffeine, processed foods, and sugary snacks can help stabilize our mood and energy levels.

4. Stress Management and Relaxation Techniques: Incorporating stress management techniques into our daily routine can help us unwind and recharge. Deep breathing exercises, progressive muscle relaxation, and aromatherapy are just a few examples of effective relaxation techniques. Finding activities we enjoy, such as painting, reading, or gardening, can also provide a much-needed break from daily stressors.

5. Sleep and Relaxation: Sleep deprivation can significantly impact our stress levels and overall well-being. Establishing a consistent sleep routine and creating a relaxing bedtime environment can help improve the quality of our sleep. Avoiding electronic devices before bed, practicing relaxation techniques, and creating a comfortable sleep environment are essential for a good night's rest.

By implementing these effective stress management techniques into our lives, we can take control of our emotional well-being and nurture our mental health. Remember, stress is a natural part of life, but how we choose to manage it can make all the difference. Prioritizing self-care and incorporating these techniques into our daily routine is a vital step towards achieving a healthier and more fulfilling life for everyone.

Relaxation Strategies for Mental Well-being

In today's fast-paced and stress-filled world, taking care of our mental well-being is more important than ever. Our mental health impacts every aspect of our lives, from our relationships and work performance to our physical health. To nurture our emotional well-being, it is essential to incorporate relaxation strategies into our daily routines.

One effective approach to promoting mental well-being is practicing mindfulness and meditation. These practices involve bringing our attention to the present moment, cultivating self-awareness, and embracing a non-judgmental attitude. By engaging in mindfulness and meditation exercises, we can reduce stress, enhance concentration, and improve overall mental clarity. Whether it's taking a few minutes to focus on our breath or participating in guided meditation sessions, these practices can significantly contribute to our mental well-being.

In addition to mindfulness and meditation, physical activity plays a crucial role in maintaining mental health. Regular exercise not only improves physical fitness but also releases endorphins, the "feel-good" hormones. Engaging in activities such as walking, jogging, or yoga not only helps to reduce stress but also boosts our mood and promotes better sleep. By incorporating fitness and exercise into our daily routines, we can enhance our overall emotional well-being.

Nutrition and healthy eating also play a vital role in supporting mental health. Consuming a balanced diet rich in fruits, vegetables, whole grains, and lean proteins provides our bodies with the necessary nutrients to function optimally. Certain foods, such as fatty fish, nuts, and dark chocolate, contain nutrients that promote brain health and can positively impact our mood. By making mindful choices about what we eat, we can nourish our bodies and minds.

Stress management and relaxation techniques are essential tools for maintaining mental well-being. Engaging in activities such as deep breathing exercises, progressive muscle relaxation, or listening to calming music can help reduce stress levels and promote relaxation. Taking breaks, practicing self-care, and setting boundaries are also crucial in managing stress effectively. By incorporating these techniques into our daily lives, we can better cope with stressors and improve our mental well-being.

Finally, prioritizing quality sleep is essential for our mental health. Establishing a consistent sleep routine, creating a comfortable sleep environment, and practicing relaxation techniques before bed can improve sleep quality. Sufficient sleep not only allows our bodies to rest and recover but also enhances cognitive function, emotional regulation, and overall mental well-being.

By incorporating relaxation strategies into our lives, we can nurture our mental well-being and lead happier, healthier lives. Whether through mindfulness and meditation, fitness and exercise, nutrition, stress management, or quality sleep, everyone can benefit from these practices. Taking care of our mental health is a lifelong journey, and by investing in ourselves, we can thrive in all aspects of life.

Chapter 7: Sleep and Relaxation

The Importance of Quality Sleep

In today's fast-paced world, it is easy to overlook the importance of quality sleep. We often prioritize work, socializing, and other activities over getting a good night's rest. However, sleep is not just a luxury, but a fundamental need for our overall well-being. It is a key pillar of good mental health and emotional well-being. In this subchapter, we will delve into why quality sleep is so crucial for everyone.

Sleep plays a vital role in maintaining our physical health. During sleep, our bodies repair and rejuvenate themselves. It is during this time that our immune system strengthens, enabling us to fight off illnesses more effectively. Lack of sleep, on the other hand, weakens our immune system, making us more susceptible to infections and diseases.

Furthermore, quality sleep is essential for our mental health. It is during sleep that our brains process and consolidate information, enhancing our memory and cognitive functions. It also helps regulate our emotions, keeping us more stable and resilient in the face of stressors. Conversely, sleep deprivation can lead to mood swings, irritability, and difficulty in controlling emotions.

For those invested in health and wellness, prioritizing quality sleep is crucial. It directly impacts our physical fitness and exercise routine. Without adequate rest, our bodies are unable to recover from workouts and build muscle effectively. Additionally, sleep deprivation can impair our coordination and reaction time, increasing the risk of accidents during physical activities.

Nutrition and healthy eating enthusiasts should also recognize the importance of sleep. Lack of sleep disrupts our hormones, leading to increased hunger and cravings for unhealthy foods. It also affects our metabolism, making it harder to maintain a healthy weight. On the other hand, getting enough sleep helps regulate our appetite and supports a balanced diet.

Finally, for those seeking stress management and relaxation techniques, quality sleep is a crucial component. It allows our bodies and minds to recharge, reducing the negative impact of stress on our mental and physical well-being. Sleep deprivation, on the other hand, amplifies stress levels and can lead to a vicious cycle of heightened anxiety and sleeplessness.

In conclusion, quality sleep is of utmost importance for everyone, regardless of their niche or interests. It is the foundation of good mental health, physical well-being, and emotional stability. By prioritizing sleep, we can enhance our overall quality of life and unlock our full potential. So, let us all make a commitment to give ourselves the gift of a good night's sleep.

Establishing Healthy Sleep Habits

Getting a good night's sleep is crucial for our overall well-being. It not only helps us feel refreshed and energized, but it also plays a vital role in maintaining good mental health and emotional well-being. In this subchapter, we will delve into the importance of establishing healthy sleep habits and explore various strategies to achieve a restful night's sleep.

Sleep is often overlooked in our busy lives, but it is essential for our physical and mental health. Lack of quality sleep can lead to a range of health issues, including increased stress levels, decreased cognitive function, and weakened immune system. Therefore, it is crucial for everyone to prioritize their sleep and establish healthy habits that promote restful nights.

One of the first steps in establishing healthy sleep habits is to maintain a consistent sleep schedule. Going to bed and waking up at the same time every day, even on weekends, helps regulate our body's internal clock and promotes better sleep quality. Additionally, creating a relaxing bedtime routine can signal our brain and body that it's time to unwind and prepare for sleep. This routine can include activities such as reading a book, taking a warm bath, or practicing relaxation techniques like deep breathing or meditation.

Another important aspect of healthy sleep habits is creating a sleep-friendly environment. Ensure your bedroom is cool, dark, and quiet to optimize your sleep environment. Remove any electronic devices that emit blue light, as it can disrupt your natural sleep-wake cycle. Investing in a comfortable mattress and pillows can also significantly improve your sleep quality.

In addition to these lifestyle changes, it's crucial to prioritize self-care practices that support a good night's sleep. Regular exercise during the day can help promote better sleep, but avoid intense workouts close to bedtime as it can stimulate your body and make it difficult to fall asleep. It's also important to be mindful of your caffeine and alcohol intake, as these substances can interfere with your sleep patterns.

By establishing healthy sleep habits, you can significantly improve your overall well-being. Remember, quality sleep is not a luxury but a necessity for everyone. Prioritize your sleep, create a sleep-friendly environment, and incorporate relaxation techniques into your bedtime routine. With dedication and consistency, you can achieve restful nights and wake up each day feeling rejuvenated and ready to take on the world.

Relaxation Techniques for Better Sleep

In today's fast-paced world, getting a good night's sleep has become increasingly challenging for many people. The constant demands of work, family, and other responsibilities often leave us feeling stressed and anxious, making it difficult to unwind and fall asleep easily. However, incorporating relaxation techniques into our daily routine can greatly improve our sleep quality and overall well-being.

One effective technique for better sleep is practicing mindfulness and meditation. By focusing on the present moment and quieting the mind, we can alleviate stress and promote relaxation. Mindfulness exercises, such as deep breathing or body scan meditation, can be practiced before bedtime to release tension and prepare the body for sleep. By cultivating a regular mindfulness practice, we can train our minds to let go of racing thoughts and create a peaceful state conducive to restful sleep.

Another essential aspect of better sleep is physical fitness and exercise. Engaging in regular physical activity not only improves our physical health but also promotes better sleep. Exercise helps release endorphins, which are natural mood-boosting chemicals that aid relaxation and reduce anxiety. However, it's important to avoid exercising too close to bedtime, as it can increase alertness and make it harder to fall asleep. Aim to finish your workout at least a few hours before bedtime to allow your body time to wind down.

Nutrition and healthy eating habits also play a significant role in our sleep quality. Avoid consuming heavy meals or stimulants, such as caffeine or nicotine, close to bedtime. Instead, opt for lighter, balanced meals that include sleep-promoting foods, such as whole grains, lean proteins, and foods rich in tryptophan, like turkey or bananas. Additionally, incorporating herbal teas like chamomile or lavender before bed can have a calming effect on the body and promote better sleep.

Stress management and relaxation techniques are vital components of achieving restful sleep. Engaging in activities that help us unwind, such as taking a warm bath, practicing gentle stretching or yoga, or listening to soothing music, can help reduce stress levels and prepare our minds for sleep. Creating a bedtime routine that includes these relaxation techniques signals to our body that it's time to relax and promotes a more restorative sleep.

Prioritizing mental health and emotional well-being is crucial for better sleep. Finding healthy ways to cope with stress, such as journaling, talking to a trusted friend or therapist, or engaging in hobbies or activities that bring joy, can help create a positive mindset and reduce sleep disturbances. Taking care of our mental health ultimately leads to improved sleep and overall well-being.

In conclusion, incorporating relaxation techniques into our daily lives is essential for better sleep. By practicing mindfulness and meditation, engaging in regular exercise, adopting healthy eating habits, managing stress, and prioritizing mental health, we can create an optimal environment for restful sleep. Remember, a good night's sleep is not only a luxury but a necessity for everyone's physical and emotional well-being.

Chapter 8: Seeking Help and Support

Recognizing When to Seek Professional Help

In today's fast-paced world, it is essential to prioritize our mental health and emotional well-being. While many of us may try to manage our mental health on our own, there are times when seeking professional help becomes necessary. Understanding when to reach out for assistance is crucial in maintaining our overall well-being.

One of the first signs that indicate the need for professional help is when our usual coping mechanisms fail to bring relief. If you find yourself constantly overwhelmed, unable to concentrate, or experience a persistent feeling of sadness or anxiety, it may be time to seek guidance from a mental health professional. They can help you explore the underlying causes of your distress and develop effective strategies to overcome them.

Another crucial factor to consider is when your mental health begins to interfere with your daily life and relationships. If you notice a significant decline in your performance at work or school, difficulty maintaining relationships, or a loss of interest in activities you once enjoyed, it may be a sign that professional help is needed. Seeking assistance can help you regain control of your life and foster healthier connections with those around you.

Additionally, if you have experienced a traumatic event or are struggling with unresolved past issues, professional help can provide the necessary support for healing and growth. Trauma can have a lasting impact on our mental health, and seeking professional guidance can help us navigate the road to recovery.

It is important to remember that seeking professional help is not a sign of weakness but rather an act of strength and self-care. Mental health professionals are trained to provide evidence-based treatments and support tailored to your specific needs. They can offer valuable insights, coping strategies, and a safe space for you to express your feelings without judgment.

Remember, you don't have to face your mental health challenges alone. Seeking professional help is a proactive step towards nurturing your emotional well-being. By recognizing when to seek assistance, you are taking an active role in your mental health journey and investing in your overall happiness and quality of life.

If you or someone you know is struggling with their mental health, do not hesitate to reach out to a mental health professional. They are here to support you on your path to recovery.

Different Mental Health Professionals and Their Roles

When it comes to mental health, there is a wide range of professionals who can provide support and guidance. Each mental health professional has their own unique role and expertise, ensuring that individuals receive the specific care they need. In this subchapter, we will explore some of the different mental health professionals and the invaluable roles they play in nurturing emotional well-being for all.

Psychiatrists are medical doctors who specialize in mental health. They are trained to diagnose and treat mental illnesses using a combination of therapy and medication. Psychiatrists play a crucial role in managing severe mental health conditions such as bipolar disorder and schizophrenia.

Psychologists are experts in human behavior and the mind. They employ various therapeutic techniques to help individuals overcome challenges and improve their mental well-being. Psychologists do not prescribe medication but focus on psychotherapy, counseling, and behavior modification.

Counselors or therapists offer talk therapy to individuals dealing with a range of mental health issues. They provide a safe and supportive environment for individuals to discuss their problems and develop coping strategies. Counselors may specialize in areas such as marriage and family therapy, addiction counseling, or trauma counseling.

Social workers play a vital role in connecting individuals with the necessary resources and support systems. They assist individuals in navigating the complex healthcare system and provide counseling services. Social workers also address social issues that may impact mental health, such as poverty, housing, and access to healthcare.

Psychiatric nurses work closely with psychiatrists to provide comprehensive care to patients. They administer medication, monitor treatment plans, and educate patients and their families about mental health conditions. Psychiatric nurses play an essential role in the ongoing management of mental health disorders.

Peer support specialists are individuals who have personal experience with mental health challenges and are trained to provide support to others going through similar struggles. They offer empathy, guidance, and encouragement based on their own lived experiences, fostering a sense of hope and connection.

These mental health professionals, along with many others, form a multidisciplinary team dedicated to promoting emotional well-being for all. By understanding the roles and expertise of each professional, individuals can make informed decisions about seeking the right support. Remember, seeking help is a sign of strength, and there is a whole network of professionals ready to support you on your mental health journey.

Building a Supportive Network

In today's fast-paced and interconnected world, the importance of building a supportive network cannot be overstated. Whether you are striving for better mental health, emotional well-being, or overall physical wellness, having a strong support system can make a world of difference. This subchapter delves into the significance of cultivating a supportive network and provides practical tips to help you foster meaningful connections.

Human beings are social creatures by nature, and we thrive when we have a network of individuals who genuinely care about our well-being. A supportive network can consist of family members, friends, colleagues, or even online communities that share common interests and goals. These connections play a crucial role in our mental health, providing emotional support, encouragement, and a sense of belonging.

When it comes to health and wellness, a supportive network can offer invaluable guidance and motivation. Whether you are embarking on a fitness journey, adopting a healthier diet, or exploring mindfulness and meditation practices, having like-minded individuals by your side can make the process more enjoyable and sustainable. They can hold you accountable, celebrate your successes, and provide a listening ear during challenging times.

Stress management and relaxation techniques are essential components of maintaining good mental health. Building a supportive network can ensure you have a safe space to share your stressors and explore effective coping strategies. Surrounding yourself with individuals who understand and empathize with your struggles can provide immense comfort and reassurance.

Furthermore, sleep and relaxation are vital for our overall well-being. A supportive network can help create an environment conducive to restful sleep by offering tips, advice, and even sharing sleep-related resources. They can also encourage you to prioritize relaxation and self-care, reminding you of the importance of taking time for yourself.

Building a supportive network requires effort and investment, but the rewards are immeasurable. Actively seek out individuals who share your interests and values, join community groups, and engage in activities that align with your passions. Foster relationships based on trust, open communication, and mutual support. Remember, a supportive network is about both giving and receiving, so be willing to offer your support to others as well.

In conclusion, building a supportive network is a crucial aspect of nurturing emotional well-being for everyone. Whether it's for health and wellness, mindfulness and meditation, fitness and exercise, nutrition and healthy eating, stress management and relaxation techniques, mental health and emotional well-being, or sleep and relaxation, a strong support system can provide the foundation for a happier, healthier life. Take the first step today and start cultivating meaningful connections that will uplift and support you on your journey towards well-being.

Chapter 9: Promoting Mental Health in Everyday Life

Creating a Positive and Supportive Environment

In today's fast-paced world, where stress and anxiety have become a common part of our lives, it is essential to prioritize our mental health and emotional well-being. Creating a positive and supportive environment can play a significant role in nurturing our emotional well-being and ensuring a healthy and balanced life. This subchapter explores various strategies and techniques that can help everyone, regardless of their background or lifestyle, to foster a positive and supportive environment.

One of the fundamental pillars of creating a positive environment is promoting health and wellness. Prioritizing physical and mental well-being is crucial for maintaining a positive mindset. Incorporating mindfulness and meditation practices into daily routines can help individuals become more self-aware and centered, reducing stress and promoting overall well-being. Additionally, engaging in regular fitness and exercise activities not only improves physical health but also releases endorphins, which boost mood and positivity.

Another essential aspect of a positive environment is nutrition and healthy eating. Consuming a balanced diet rich in nutrients and vitamins not only supports physical health but also has a significant impact on mental well-being. Educating oneself about nutrition and making conscious choices about what we eat can greatly contribute to a positive mindset.

Stress management and relaxation techniques also play a vital role in fostering a supportive environment. Learning effective stress management strategies such as deep breathing exercises, journaling, or engaging in hobbies can help individuals cope with daily stressors and promote emotional well-being. Additionally, incorporating relaxation techniques such as yoga or aromatherapy can create a calming atmosphere and promote a positive mindset.

Sleep and relaxation are often overlooked aspects of mental health and emotional well-being. Creating a sleep routine that prioritizes restful and uninterrupted sleep is essential for recharging our minds and bodies. Establishing a soothing environment in the bedroom, practicing relaxation techniques before bed, and maintaining a consistent sleep schedule can contribute to a positive and supportive environment.

In conclusion, creating a positive and supportive environment is crucial for nurturing emotional well-being for all. By incorporating strategies such as mindfulness and meditation, promoting health and wellness, focusing on nutrition, managing stress, and prioritizing sleep, individuals can cultivate a positive mindset and foster emotional well-being. Regardless of one's background or lifestyle, everyone can benefit from creating an environment that supports mental health and emotional well-being.

Cultivating Resilience and Coping Skills

In today's fast-paced and demanding world, it is essential to develop resilience and coping skills to navigate the challenges that life throws our way. Resilience refers to our ability to bounce back from setbacks, adapt to change, and thrive in the face of adversity. This subchapter explores various strategies and techniques to cultivate resilience and enhance our coping skills, fostering mental well-being and emotional balance.

One effective way to cultivate resilience is through mindfulness and meditation practices. Mindfulness teaches us to be present in the moment, allowing us to observe and accept our thoughts and emotions without judgment. By cultivating this non-reactive awareness, we can develop a greater sense of resilience, enabling us to respond to stressors with clarity and composure.

Physical fitness and exercise also play a vital role in building resilience. Regular physical activity not only improves our physical health but also boosts our mental well-being. Engaging in activities like running, yoga, or strength training releases endorphins, the feel-good hormones, which help alleviate stress and anxiety. Moreover, exercise provides an opportunity to challenge ourselves, building mental resilience along with physical strength.

Nutrition and healthy eating habits are crucial for maintaining a balanced state of mind. A well-nourished body supports a healthy brain, improving our ability to cope with stress and regulate emotions. Incorporating whole foods, such as fruits, vegetables, whole grains, and lean proteins, into our diet can provide the necessary nutrients to support optimal brain function and emotional well-being.

Stress management and relaxation techniques are essential tools for building resilience. Learning to recognize and manage stress effectively can prevent it from overwhelming us. Techniques such as deep breathing exercises, progressive muscle relaxation, or engaging in hobbies and activities we enjoy can help us relax and recharge, fostering resilience in the face of adversity.

Furthermore, prioritizing mental health and emotional well-being is vital for cultivating resilience. Seeking support from friends, family, or professionals, and engaging in therapy or counseling, can provide valuable insights and coping mechanisms. Taking care of our mental health should be viewed as a proactive and ongoing process, just like maintaining our physical health.

Lastly, adequate sleep and relaxation are fundamental for building resilience. A good night's rest rejuvenates our body and mind, allowing us to face challenges with clarity and focus. Incorporating relaxation techniques, such as meditation or reading, into our bedtime routine can help promote deep, restorative sleep.

By cultivating resilience and enhancing coping skills through mindfulness, exercise, nutrition, stress management, mental health support, and sleep, we can nurture our emotional well-being and thrive in all aspects of life. Remember, resilience is not about avoiding adversity but about equipping ourselves with the tools to face it head-on and emerge stronger.

Taking Care of Your Mental Health at Work

In today's fast-paced and demanding world, taking care of your mental health is crucial, especially in the workplace where stress levels can skyrocket. This subchapter will provide valuable insights and practical tips on how to nurture your emotional well-being at work. Whether you are an employee, employer, or self-employed, this information will be beneficial for everyone.

One of the key aspects of maintaining good mental health at work is practicing mindfulness and meditation. Incorporating these practices into your daily routine can help you stay focused, reduce stress, and enhance your overall well-being. Taking a few minutes each day to quiet your mind and focus on the present moment can have a profound impact on your mental health.

Physical fitness and exercise also play a significant role in promoting mental well-being. Regular physical activity not only boosts your mood but also improves cognitive function and reduces anxiety and depression. Whether it's going for a walk during your lunch break, taking the stairs instead of the elevator, or participating in a fitness class after work, finding ways to incorporate movement into your day is crucial.

Nutrition and healthy eating are often overlooked when it comes to mental health, but they are equally important. Fueling your body with nutritious foods can help stabilize your mood, improve concentration, and increase energy levels. Incorporating whole grains, fruits, vegetables, lean proteins, and healthy fats into your diet can make a significant difference in how you feel both physically and mentally.

Managing stress and practicing relaxation techniques are essential skills for maintaining mental well-being. Learning how to identify and manage stressors at work can help prevent burnout and improve your overall quality of life. Techniques such as deep breathing exercises, progressive muscle relaxation, and guided imagery can help you relax and reduce stress levels, even in the midst of a hectic workday.

Prioritizing mental health and emotional well-being also involves getting enough sleep and relaxation. Adequate sleep is crucial for maintaining mental clarity, emotional stability, and overall health. Establishing a consistent sleep routine and creating a relaxing sleep environment can significantly improve the quality of your sleep and, consequently, your mental well-being.

In conclusion, taking care of your mental health at work is vital for everyone, regardless of their profession or position. Incorporating practices such as mindfulness and meditation, physical fitness and exercise, nutrition and healthy eating, stress management and relaxation techniques, as well as prioritizing sleep and relaxation, can have a transformative effect on your emotional well-being. By nurturing your mental health, you can thrive in the workplace and lead a more fulfilling and balanced life.

Chapter 10: Mental Health and Relationships

Nurturing Healthy Relationships for Emotional Well-being

Building and maintaining healthy relationships is crucial for our emotional well-being. Whether it's with family, friends, or romantic partners, these connections contribute significantly to our overall happiness and mental health. In this subchapter, we will explore the importance of nurturing healthy relationships and provide practical tips on how to cultivate and maintain them.

Strong relationships have a profound impact on our mental health and emotional well-being. They provide a sense of belonging, support, and love, which are essential for our overall happiness. Having someone to share our joys and sorrows, to listen and empathize with us, can alleviate stress and strengthen our resilience. Positive relationships also enhance our self-esteem and boost our confidence, fostering a sense of security and stability in our lives.

To nurture healthy relationships, it is essential to prioritize effective communication. Active listening, expressing feelings and needs openly, and practicing empathy are key components of successful communication. By actively listening to others, we show respect and create a safe space for open dialogue. Sharing our thoughts and emotions honestly allows for a deeper connection and understanding.

Additionally, setting boundaries is crucial for maintaining healthy relationships. Communicating our limits and respecting the boundaries of others fosters mutual respect and prevents conflicts. It is important to remember that healthy relationships are based on equality and shared decision-making, where both parties feel valued and heard.

Practicing gratitude and appreciation is another significant aspect of nurturing healthy relationships. Expressing gratitude for the presence and support of our loved ones strengthens the bond and fosters positivity. Simple acts of kindness, such as a heartfelt thank-you note or a small gesture of appreciation, can go a long way in maintaining strong relationships.

Finally, investing time and effort in building and maintaining relationships is essential. Engaging in activities together, such as shared hobbies or quality time, strengthens the connection and creates lasting memories. Regularly checking in with our loved ones, even during busy periods, shows care and commitment.

In conclusion, nurturing healthy relationships is vital for our emotional well-being. By prioritizing effective communication, setting boundaries, practicing gratitude, and investing time and effort, we can cultivate and maintain strong connections with our loved ones. These relationships provide us with the support, love, and belonging we need to lead fulfilling lives. So, let's cherish and nurture our relationships, as they are the foundation of our emotional well-being.

Communication and Conflict Resolution

Effective communication is the cornerstone of every healthy relationship, be it personal or professional. It forms the foundation for understanding, empathy, and cooperation. In the realm of mental health and emotional well-being, the significance of communication cannot be overstated. This subchapter aims to explore the vital role that communication plays in resolving conflicts and promoting overall emotional well-being.

Conflict is an inevitable part of life, but how we communicate and resolve it can make all the difference. When conflict arises, it often stems from misunderstandings, differing perspectives, or unmet needs. By developing strong communication skills, we can navigate these conflicts with grace and compassion.

One key aspect of effective communication is active listening. This involves giving our full attention to the other person, setting aside any preconceived notions or judgments, and truly trying to understand their perspective. Active listening allows us to validate their feelings, which can go a long way in defusing tension and finding common ground.

Alongside active listening, assertive communication is vital in conflict resolution. Assertiveness means expressing our needs, thoughts, and feelings in a clear, direct, and respectful manner. By being assertive, we can avoid passive-aggressive behavior or explosive outbursts that only escalate conflicts. It enables us to communicate our boundaries effectively and work towards mutually beneficial solutions.

In the context of conflict resolution, it is crucial to remember that communication is a two-way street. It requires both parties to engage in dialogue openly and honestly. This means being willing to compromise, empathize, and find win-win solutions that address the underlying issues.

Moreover, effective communication is not limited to verbal interactions alone. Nonverbal cues, such as body language and facial expressions, can convey a wealth of information. Being mindful of these nonverbal cues allows us to better understand others and respond in a way that fosters understanding and connection.

In conclusion, communication and conflict resolution are essential skills for everyone seeking to nurture their mental health and emotional well-being. By developing effective communication skills, we can address conflicts with empathy, respect, and understanding. This subchapter aims to equip individuals with the tools they need to engage in healthy communication, fostering stronger relationships and promoting overall well-being. Whether in the realms of health and wellness, mindfulness and meditation, fitness and exercise, nutrition and healthy eating, stress management and relaxation techniques, or sleep and relaxation, effective communication is a universal skill that can benefit us all.

Supportive Strategies for Loved Ones with Mental Health Issues

When a loved one is struggling with mental health issues, it can be challenging to know how to provide the right support. However, with the right strategies, you can create a nurturing environment that promotes their emotional well-being. In this subchapter, we will explore various supportive techniques that can benefit both you and your loved one.

Firstly, it is crucial to educate yourself about mental health and the specific condition your loved one is facing. By understanding the symptoms, treatment options, and possible triggers, you can offer informed support. Consider attending support groups or seeking professional advice to gain more knowledge about their condition.

Open and honest communication is another essential strategy. Encourage your loved one to express their feelings and concerns without judgment. Create a safe space where they can share their experiences and be heard. Active listening and empathy can go a long way in providing the emotional support they need.

Incorporating mindfulness and meditation practices into your daily routine can greatly benefit both you and your loved one's mental health. Engaging in mindful activities such as yoga or deep breathing exercises can help reduce stress and promote relaxation. Encourage your loved one to join you in these practices or suggest mindfulness apps or guided meditation recordings they can explore on their own.

Physical health plays a vital role in mental well-being. Encourage your loved one to engage in regular exercise or join you in fitness activities. Exercise releases endorphins, which can boost their mood and reduce symptoms of anxiety or depression. Additionally, focus on promoting a balanced diet and healthy eating habits. Providing nutritious meals and avoiding excessive caffeine or refined sugars can positively impact their overall well-being.

Managing stress is crucial for mental health. Help your loved one identify stress triggers and develop effective coping mechanisms. Encourage them to engage in activities they enjoy, such as hobbies or creative outlets, to reduce stress levels. Introduce relaxation techniques such as deep breathing exercises or guided imagery to help them find moments of calmness.

Lastly, prioritize sleep and relaxation. Ensure your loved one is getting enough rest by creating a soothing bedtime routine. Encourage them to establish a regular sleep schedule and create a comfortable sleep environment. Proper sleep hygiene is essential for mental health and emotional well-being.

In conclusion, supporting a loved one with mental health issues requires a compassionate and informed approach. By educating yourself, fostering open communication, practicing mindfulness, promoting physical health, managing stress, and prioritizing sleep, you can provide the support they need to navigate their mental health journey. Remember, your support can make a significant difference in their overall well-being.

Chapter 11: Overcoming Stigma and Advocacy

Understanding Mental Health Stigma

Mental Health Matters: Nurturing Emotional Well-being for All

In today's fast-paced and demanding world, mental health is an issue that affects everyone. Whether you are a health and wellness enthusiast, a mindfulness and meditation practitioner, a fitness and exercise enthusiast, a nutrition and healthy eating advocate, or someone seeking stress management and relaxation techniques, understanding mental health stigma is crucial for overall well-being. This subchapter aims to shed light on the importance of addressing mental health stigma and its impact on mental health and emotional well-being.

Mental health stigma refers to the negative attitudes, beliefs, and stereotypes surrounding mental health conditions. These misconceptions often lead to discrimination, social exclusion, and the reluctance to seek help or support. It is prevalent in society, with many individuals facing judgment, ridicule, and isolation due to their mental health struggles. This stigma creates barriers to accessing appropriate care and support, perpetuating a cycle of suffering and hindering recovery.

For those passionate about health and wellness, mental health stigma should be considered an integral part of overall well-being. Physical health is often prioritized, while mental health is neglected or dismissed. However, neglecting mental health can have severe consequences on physical health and vice versa. Recognizing and addressing mental health stigma can help create a more holistic approach to well-being, where mental and physical health are regarded as equally important.

Mindfulness and meditation practitioners understand the power of non-judgmental awareness and compassion. By understanding mental health stigma, they can cultivate empathy and support those affected by mental health conditions. Breaking down the barriers caused by stigma allows individuals to fully embrace mindfulness and meditation practices, leading to greater emotional well-being.

Fitness and exercise enthusiasts often focus on the physical benefits of staying active. However, exercise has numerous mental health benefits as well. By educating themselves about mental health stigma, they can create inclusive environments where individuals feel comfortable and safe to engage in physical activities without fear of judgment or discrimination.

Nutrition and healthy eating advocates recognize the impact of diet on overall well-being. Understanding mental health stigma enables them to address the emotional aspects of nutrition, supporting individuals who may struggle with disordered eating or other mental health conditions.

Stress management and relaxation techniques play a vital role in maintaining mental health. By acknowledging mental health stigma, practitioners can enhance their techniques to foster a more inclusive and understanding environment, allowing individuals to seek help and support without fear of judgment.

In conclusion, understanding mental health stigma is essential for everyone interested in promoting mental health and emotional well-being. By addressing stigma, we can create a society where individuals feel empowered to seek help, support, and engage in practices that nurture their mental health. Let us embrace compassion, empathy, and understanding, breaking down the barriers that hinder the path to emotional well-being for all.

Challenging Stigma through Education and Awareness

In today's fast-paced and interconnected world, mental health has become an increasingly important topic of discussion. Despite the progress made in recent years, there is still a pervasive stigma surrounding mental health that prevents many individuals from seeking the help they need. However, education and awareness can play a crucial role in challenging this stigma and promoting emotional well-being for all.

The subchapter "Challenging Stigma through Education and Awareness" aims to shed light on the significance of understanding and addressing mental health issues. It is addressed to everyone, as mental health impacts people from all walks of life. Whether you are interested in health and wellness, mindfulness and meditation, fitness and exercise, nutrition and healthy eating, stress management and relaxation techniques, or simply enhancing your mental well-being, this subchapter is for you.

Education and awareness are key components in breaking down the barriers associated with mental health stigma. By providing accurate information, dispelling myths, and promoting open and honest conversations, we can create a more compassionate and inclusive society. The subchapter emphasizes the importance of destigmatizing mental health conditions and encouraging individuals to seek help without fear or shame.

Furthermore, this subchapter explores various strategies to challenge stigma and promote mental health in different aspects of life. It delves into the significance of incorporating mindfulness and meditation practices into our daily routines to reduce stress and improve overall well-being. It also highlights the link between physical fitness, nutrition, and mental health, offering tips on how to maintain a healthy lifestyle that supports emotional well-being.

Additionally, the subchapter addresses stress management and relaxation techniques that can be incorporated into our busy lives, helping us to find balance and reduce the risk of mental health challenges. It also emphasizes the importance of quality sleep and provides practical suggestions for improving sleep patterns.

In conclusion, "Challenging Stigma through Education and Awareness" is a subchapter that aims to empower individuals in their journey towards emotional well-being. It offers valuable insights and practical strategies for everyone, regardless of their interests or niches. By embracing education and awareness, we can collectively challenge the stigma surrounding mental health and create a society that nurtures and supports the emotional well-being of all its members.

Becoming an Advocate for Mental Health

In today's fast-paced and demanding world, taking care of our mental health has never been more important. Mental health issues can affect anyone, regardless of age, gender, or background. It is essential that we all become advocates for mental health to foster emotional well-being for ourselves and those around us. This subchapter aims to provide practical tips and strategies for everyone, regardless of their interests or niches, to become advocates for mental health.

Health and wellness enthusiasts can integrate mental health into their holistic well-being routine. It is crucial to recognize the interconnectedness of physical and mental health. Engaging in regular exercise, practicing mindfulness and meditation, and adopting a nutritious diet are all effective ways to support mental well-being.

Mindfulness and meditation practitioners can extend their practice beyond their personal growth and use it to advocate for mental health. By sharing their experiences and knowledge, they can inspire others to explore mindfulness techniques and experience the positive impact on mental health.

Fitness and exercise enthusiasts can use their platform to raise awareness about the mental health benefits of physical activity. Regular exercise has been proven to reduce symptoms of anxiety and depression, boost mood, and improve overall mental well-being. By encouraging others to incorporate exercise into their daily routines, they can help promote mental health.

Nutrition and healthy eating advocates can educate others about the link between diet and mental health. A balanced and nutrient-rich diet can support brain function and positively impact mood and overall mental well-being. Sharing nutritious recipes and providing guidance on healthy eating can empower individuals to make mindful choices for their mental health.

Stress management and relaxation techniques experts can equip individuals with practical tools to manage stress and promote mental well-being. Encouraging the practice of relaxation techniques such as deep breathing exercises, progressive muscle relaxation, or journaling can help individuals cope with daily stressors and improve their mental resilience.

Finally, those interested in sleep and relaxation can emphasize the importance of quality sleep for mental health. Adequate sleep is crucial for emotional and cognitive functioning. Advocates can educate others about the significance of maintaining a consistent sleep schedule, creating a relaxing bedtime routine, and implementing good sleep hygiene practices.

By becoming advocates for mental health, we can collectively work towards nurturing emotional well-being for all. Regardless of our interests or niches, we all have the power to promote mental health and create a supportive environment that prioritizes emotional well-being. Together, we can break the stigma surrounding mental health and foster a society that values and supports mental well-being for everyone.

Chapter 12: Mental Health and Different Life Stages

Mental Health in Childhood and Adolescence

Introduction:
Mental health is a crucial aspect of overall well-being, and it is as important for children and adolescents as it is for adults. In this subchapter, we will delve into the various factors that contribute to mental health in childhood and adolescence. By understanding these factors, we can better support and nurture the emotional well-being of young individuals.

The Importance of Mental Health in Youth:
Childhood and adolescence are critical stages of development, shaping an individual's future. Positive mental health during these years promotes resilience, emotional intelligence, and the ability to cope with life's challenges. It also lays the foundation for a healthy and fulfilling adulthood.

Factors Influencing Mental Health:
Several factors contribute to mental health in childhood and adolescence. Firstly, a supportive and nurturing environment at home, school, and in the community is vital. This includes fostering positive relationships, open communication, and providing a safe space for self-expression.

Secondly, physical health plays a significant role in mental well-being. Regular exercise, a balanced diet, and adequate sleep contribute to positive mental health. Engaging in fitness and exercise activities not only boosts physical health but also helps in stress reduction and improved mood.

Thirdly, managing stress and relaxation techniques are essential skills for young individuals. Teaching mindfulness and meditation practices can aid in reducing anxiety and enhancing focus. By learning stress management techniques, adolescents can develop resilience and improve their emotional well-being.

Fourthly, promoting mental health education in schools and at home can empower young individuals to understand their emotions and seek help when needed. By providing knowledge about mental health, we can reduce stigma and create a supportive environment.

Conclusion:

Nurturing mental health in childhood and adolescence is crucial for overall well-being and lays the foundation for a healthy adulthood. By creating a supportive and nurturing environment, encouraging physical fitness, teaching stress management techniques, and promoting mental health education, we can contribute to the emotional well-being of young individuals. It is essential for everyone, including parents, educators, and society as a whole, to prioritize mental health in childhood and adolescence. By doing so, we can shape a healthier and more resilient future generation.

Addressing Mental Health in Adulthood

In the hustle and bustle of our daily lives, it is easy to overlook the importance of maintaining our mental health. However, taking care of our emotional well-being is just as crucial as our physical health. In this subchapter, we will explore the various aspects of addressing mental health in adulthood, providing valuable insights and practical tips for everyone, regardless of their age or background.

One of the fundamental pillars of mental health is mindfulness and meditation. By cultivating a sense of awareness and being present in the moment, we can effectively manage stress, reduce anxiety, and improve overall emotional well-being. Incorporating mindfulness practices into our daily routines can bring a sense of calm and clarity, allowing us to navigate the challenges of adulthood with greater resilience.

Fitness and exercise also play a vital role in maintaining mental health. Engaging in regular physical activity not only benefits our physical well-being but also has a profound impact on our mental state. Exercise releases endorphins, which are natural mood boosters, and can alleviate symptoms of depression and anxiety. By finding activities we enjoy, such as dance, yoga, or hiking, we can make exercise a joyful part of our lives while reaping its mental health benefits.

Nutrition and healthy eating are often overlooked when discussing mental health. However, our diet has a significant impact on our emotional well-being. Consuming a balanced diet rich in fruits, vegetables, whole grains, and lean proteins provides our bodies with the necessary nutrients to support brain function and promote positive mental health. Additionally, avoiding excessive caffeine, alcohol, and processed foods can help regulate mood and reduce anxiety.

Stress management and relaxation techniques are essential tools for maintaining mental health in adulthood. Learning effective coping mechanisms, such as deep breathing exercises, journaling, or engaging in creative outlets, can help us navigate the daily pressures and challenges we face. Incorporating relaxation techniques into our daily routine allows us to recharge and reduce stress levels, promoting better mental health.

Sleep and relaxation are often undervalued but are crucial for our mental well-being. Adequate sleep is essential for cognitive function, emotional regulation, and overall mental health. Establishing a regular sleep routine and creating a relaxing environment conducive to quality sleep can significantly impact our mood, energy levels, and overall mental health.

In conclusion, addressing mental health in adulthood is a multifaceted endeavor that requires attention to various aspects of our lives. By incorporating mindfulness and meditation practices, engaging in regular exercise, adopting a healthy diet, managing stress, prioritizing relaxation, and ensuring sufficient sleep, we can nurture our emotional well-being and lead fulfilling lives. Remember, taking care of our mental health is not a luxury; it is a necessity for everyone, regardless of age or background.

Promoting Emotional Well-being in Older Adults

As we age, it becomes increasingly important to prioritize our emotional well-being. Older adults often face unique challenges, such as the loss of loved ones, declining physical health, and a sense of isolation. However, there are numerous strategies that can be employed to promote emotional well-being and enhance the quality of life for older adults.

One essential aspect of emotional well-being is maintaining a healthy social network. Research has consistently shown that social connections are vital for mental and emotional health. Encourage older adults to remain active in their communities, participate in social events, and cultivate new friendships. Additionally, technology can play a significant role in combating isolation by facilitating online communication with family and friends.

Engaging in regular physical exercise is another crucial factor in promoting emotional well-being. Physical activity has been linked to a reduction in symptoms of depression and anxiety, improved cognitive function, and enhanced overall mood. Encourage older adults to find activities they enjoy, whether it's walking, swimming, yoga, or dancing. Regular exercise not only benefits physical health but also contributes to a positive mental state.

Proper nutrition is fundamental for emotional well-being. A balanced diet rich in fruits, vegetables, whole grains, and lean proteins provides the essential nutrients for optimal brain function. Encourage older adults to adopt healthy eating habits and ensure they are receiving adequate vitamin B12, omega-3 fatty acids, and antioxidants. It is crucial to stay hydrated as well, as dehydration can lead to mood disturbances and cognitive decline.

Stress management and relaxation techniques are essential for emotional well-being. Encourage older adults to incorporate activities such as meditation, deep breathing exercises, or mindfulness practices into their daily routine. These techniques can help reduce stress, enhance the ability to cope with challenges, and promote a sense of calm and well-being.

Lastly, prioritizing sleep is vital for emotional well-being. Older adults often experience changes in sleep patterns, which can negatively impact their mood and cognitive function. Encourage older adults to create a relaxing bedtime routine, establish a consistent sleep schedule, and create a sleep-friendly environment.

Promoting emotional well-being in older adults requires a holistic approach that encompasses social connections, physical activity, nutrition, stress management, and sleep. By implementing these strategies, older adults can enhance their emotional well-being, leading to a higher quality of life and improved overall health.

Chapter 13: Embracing Self-Care and Self-Compassion

The Importance of Self-Care for Mental Health

In today's fast-paced and demanding world, taking care of our mental health has become more crucial than ever before. Mental health matters, and it affects everyone, regardless of age, gender, or background. Understanding the significance of self-care is the first step towards nurturing our emotional well-being.

Self-care is about consciously taking time to prioritize and care for our own needs, both physically and mentally. It involves developing healthy habits and engaging in activities that promote relaxation, stress reduction, and overall mental well-being. While it may seem selfish to some, self-care is essential for maintaining a healthy mind and body, as it allows us to recharge, rejuvenate, and better cope with life's challenges.

One aspect of self-care that greatly impacts mental health is mindfulness and meditation. By practicing mindfulness, we can train our minds to stay present, focus on the present moment, and let go of negative thoughts. Meditation helps reduce stress, improve concentration, and promote a sense of peace and tranquility. Incorporating mindfulness and meditation into our daily routine can significantly enhance our mental well-being.

Physical health is closely intertwined with mental health. Engaging in regular fitness and exercise not only strengthens our physical body but also releases endorphins, the feel-good hormones that boost our mood. Whether it's going for a run, practicing yoga, or hitting the gym, finding a form of exercise that we enjoy is key to maintaining good mental health.

The old adage, "you are what you eat," holds true when it comes to mental health. Nutrition and healthy eating play a vital role in our emotional well-being. A balanced diet rich in fruits, vegetables, whole grains, and lean proteins provides our brain with the necessary nutrients to function optimally. Avoiding excessive caffeine, sugar, and processed foods can help stabilize our mood and energy levels.

Stress management and relaxation techniques are essential tools in self-care. Chronic stress can negatively impact mental health, leading to anxiety and depression. Learning relaxation techniques such as deep breathing exercises, progressive muscle relaxation, or engaging in hobbies can help reduce stress levels and promote a sense of calmness.

Prioritizing sleep and relaxation is crucial for mental well-being. Quality sleep allows our brain to recharge and process emotions, making us better equipped to handle daily challenges. Creating a peaceful sleep environment, establishing a bedtime routine, and practicing relaxation techniques before bed can greatly improve our sleep quality.

In conclusion, self-care is not a luxury but a necessity for maintaining good mental health. By incorporating mindfulness and meditation, fitness and exercise, nutrition and healthy eating, stress management and relaxation techniques, and prioritizing sleep and relaxation into our lives, we can nurture our emotional well-being. Remember, mental health matters, and taking care of ourselves is the first step towards leading a fulfilling and balanced life.

Self-Compassion and its Role in Emotional Well-being

In today's fast-paced and demanding world, it is crucial to prioritize our emotional well-being. Mental health matters, and one powerful tool that can help us nurture it is self-compassion. This subchapter explores the concept of self-compassion and its significant role in promoting emotional well-being.

Self-compassion can be defined as treating oneself with kindness, understanding, and acceptance, especially during times of struggle or failure. It involves recognizing our own suffering and responding with empathy and care, just as we would for a loved one. This practice not only helps us cope with difficult emotions but also cultivates resilience and a positive mindset.

Research has shown that individuals who practice self-compassion have higher levels of emotional well-being. They are more likely to experience lower levels of anxiety, depression, and stress, while also exhibiting higher levels of happiness, life satisfaction, and overall psychological well-being.

In the realm of health and wellness, self-compassion plays a vital role. By treating ourselves with kindness and understanding, we can break free from the cycle of self-criticism and self-judgment. This allows us to embrace healthier habits, such as engaging in regular exercise, adopting a balanced diet, and prioritizing adequate sleep. With self-compassion, we can approach these choices from a place of self-care rather than punishment, leading to long-lasting positive changes.

Mindfulness and meditation practices can be powerful tools in developing self-compassion. By cultivating present-moment awareness and non-judgmental acceptance, we can create a space for self-compassion to flourish. This combination helps us build resilience, manage stress, and develop a greater sense of self-acceptance.

Self-compassion also intersects with stress management and relaxation techniques. When faced with challenging situations, self-compassion allows us to respond with self-care and understanding, rather than succumbing to stress and overwhelm. By practicing self-compassion regularly, we can reduce the impact of stress on our overall well-being and enhance our ability to cope effectively.

In conclusion, self-compassion is a powerful tool that can positively impact our emotional well-being. It is a practice that can be incorporated into various aspects of our lives, including health and wellness, mindfulness and meditation, fitness and exercise, nutrition and healthy eating, stress management and relaxation techniques, mental health and emotional well-being, and sleep and relaxation. By embracing self-compassion, we can nurture our emotional well-being and create a foundation for a happier and more fulfilling life.

Incorporating Self-Care Practices into Your Daily Life

In today's fast-paced and demanding world, taking care of ourselves often takes a backseat to our never-ending to-do lists and responsibilities. However, prioritizing self-care is essential for our overall well-being. From managing stress to nurturing our emotional health, incorporating self-care practices into our daily lives is crucial for everyone.

One of the fundamental aspects of self-care is taking care of our physical health. Engaging in regular exercise and maintaining a nutritious diet is key to promoting overall wellness. Whether it's going for a jog, attending a fitness class, or practicing yoga, finding activities that we enjoy and that make us feel good can greatly contribute to our physical and mental well-being. Additionally, adopting a balanced and nutritious diet filled with whole foods, fruits, and vegetables can provide us with the energy and nutrients needed to tackle our daily tasks with vitality.

Furthermore, self-care involves prioritizing our mental health and emotional well-being. Incorporating mindfulness and meditation practices into our daily routine can help us cultivate a sense of calm and present-moment awareness. Mindfulness exercises, such as deep breathing or body scans, can be practiced anywhere and at any time, allowing us to tune into our thoughts and emotions without judgment. These practices can help reduce stress, improve focus, and enhance our overall mental clarity.

Stress management and relaxation techniques are also crucial components of self-care. Engaging in activities that help us unwind and relax can have profound effects on our mental and emotional health. Whether it's taking a warm bath, reading a book, or practicing deep relaxation techniques like progressive muscle relaxation, finding ways to decompress and let go of stress is essential for our overall well-being.

Lastly, self-care involves prioritizing quality sleep. Establishing a consistent sleep routine and creating a sleep-friendly environment can significantly improve our mood, cognitive function, and overall health. Avoiding electronic devices before bedtime, creating a calming bedtime routine, and ensuring a comfortable sleep environment are essential steps to getting restorative sleep.

Incorporating self-care practices into our daily lives is not a luxury; it is a necessity. By prioritizing our physical health, mental well-being, and emotional balance, we can lead happier, more fulfilling lives. Remember, self-care is not selfish; it is an act of self-love and self-preservation. So, let us commit to making self-care a priority and reap the benefits of a healthier and more balanced life.

Conclusion: Nurturing Your Mental Health Journey

In this book, "Mental Health Matters: Nurturing Emotional Well-being for All," we have explored the importance of mental health and provided valuable insights on how to nurture your emotional well-being. As we conclude this journey, it is crucial to reflect on the key takeaways and emphasize the significance of prioritizing mental health in our lives.

Firstly, we have learned that mental health is not limited to those who have been diagnosed with a mental illness. It is an essential aspect of everyone's life, regardless of age, gender, or background. Taking care of our mental health should be a priority for all, just like maintaining our physical health.

Throughout this book, we have discussed various niches that intersect with mental health. Health and wellness, mindfulness and meditation, fitness and exercise, nutrition and healthy eating, stress management and relaxation techniques, mental health and emotional well-being, as well as sleep and relaxation – all play a vital role in nurturing our mental health.

To nurture your mental health effectively, it is crucial to adopt a holistic approach. This involves integrating the practices and principles from various niches. Engaging in regular exercise not only benefits your physical health but also has a positive impact on your mental well-being. Similarly, incorporating mindfulness and meditation into your daily routine can help you manage stress, improve focus, and enhance emotional resilience.

In addition to these practices, maintaining a balanced and nutritious diet is essential for mental health. Research suggests that certain nutrients, such as omega-3 fatty acids and B vitamins, play a crucial role in brain function and emotional well-being. By prioritizing healthy eating habits, you are nourishing both your body and mind.

Stress management and relaxation techniques are integral components of nurturing your mental health. Learning how to identify and manage stressors in your life, as well as incorporating relaxation techniques like deep breathing exercises or engaging in activities that bring you joy and relaxation, can significantly impact your overall well-being.

Lastly, sleep is often underestimated when it comes to mental health. Quality sleep is vital for cognitive function, emotional regulation, and overall mental well-being. Prioritizing a consistent sleep schedule and creating a relaxing bedtime routine can significantly improve your sleep quality and, subsequently, your mental health.

In conclusion, nurturing your mental health is a lifelong journey that requires dedication, self-awareness, and a commitment to self-care. By integrating practices from various niches such as health and wellness, mindfulness and meditation, fitness and exercise, nutrition and healthy eating, stress management and relaxation techniques, mental health and emotional well-being, as well as sleep and relaxation, you can effectively enhance your emotional well-being and lead a more fulfilling life. Remember, your mental health matters, and you deserve to prioritize it.

In "Mental Health Matters: Nurturing Emotional Well-being for All," we aim to create a comprehensive guide that addresses the diverse needs of our readers. Whether you are interested in health and wellness, mindfulness and meditation, fitness and exercise, nutrition and healthy eating, stress management and relaxation techniques, mental health and emotional well-being, or sleep and relaxation, this book has something for everyone.

Understanding that each individual has their unique concerns and preferences, we have taken utmost care to provide information that can be customized to suit your needs. We encourage you to explore the chapters and sub-chapters that resonate most with your interests and goals, as you embark on a journey towards improved mental health and emotional well-being.

For those interested in health and wellness, we delve into a variety of topics such as the importance of self-care, the impact of physical activity on mental health, and techniques to maintain a healthy lifestyle. We provide practical tips and advice that can easily be incorporated into your daily routine.

Mindfulness and meditation enthusiasts will find a wealth of information on how to cultivate mindfulness, the benefits of meditation, and techniques for stress reduction and relaxation. We explore different meditation practices and offer guidance on incorporating mindfulness into your daily life.

Fitness and exercise enthusiasts can discover the connection between physical activity and mental well-being. We discuss the role of exercise in managing stress, improving mood, and boosting overall mental health. Additionally, we provide exercise recommendations and tips for staying motivated.

Our chapter on nutrition and healthy eating provides insights into the impact of diet on mental health. We explore the relationship between certain nutrients and brain function, and offer practical suggestions for incorporating nutritious foods into your diet.

Stress management and relaxation techniques are essential in our fast-paced world, and we provide a range of strategies to help you effectively manage stress. From deep breathing exercises to progressive muscle relaxation techniques, you'll find a variety of tools to help you unwind and find inner peace.

Of course, mental health and emotional well-being are at the core of this book. We cover various aspects of mental health, including common mental health conditions, strategies for maintaining emotional balance, and resources for seeking professional help when needed.

Lastly, we recognize the importance of sleep and relaxation for overall well-being. In this chapter, we discuss the impact of sleep on mental health, provide tips for improving sleep quality, and explore relaxation techniques that promote restful nights.

Remember, this book is designed to cater to your specific needs and interests. Feel free to explore the chapters and sub-chapters that resonate with you, and tailor the information to fit your unique circumstances. We believe that by doing so, you'll find the guidance and support necessary to nurture your emotional well-being and promote a healthy, fulfilling life.